I0701631

new words

{young poets vol 1}

a trans* & gender-expansive press

new words {press}
New York, NY
www.newwordspress.com | @newwordspress

new words {press} is a sponsored project of Fractured Atlas, a non-profit arts service organization. Our mission is to elevate emerging and established trans* and gender-expansive poetic voices, to build community, and share knowledge.

ISBN: 979-8-9903488-2-0
Cover art by Baran Lotfollahi on Unsplash
Cover Layout by brooklyn baggett
Typesetting by new words {press}
Font: Bondoni 72 Oldstyle, Baskerville

Thank you for supporting this special issue of *new words*. We are dedicated to raising the voices of trans and gender-expansive poets and doing so through a more inclusive, less gatekeeping, model.

new words {press} is self-funded and volunteer-based. Please consider purchasing a subsciption. You can also donate (https://fundraising.fracturedatlas.org/new-words-press/general_support). Please consider donating and/or sharing it with others.

{ staff }

brooklyn baggett (she/her)
managing editor

GUEST READERS

Luna Yin (she/they) is a 16-year-old writer caught between cultures and questions. When they aren't escaping into words and stories, they spend their time at the piano.

EG Harcourt is an artist who uses words and images to explore and construct his identity as an Asian trans man. Most of his work includes themes of religion, cultural identity, and social alienation.

S.R. Nickoloff Warren's (she/they) work has been published in *Room to Grow*, *Quarantine Content*, *Honeysuckle Media*, and *Letting Go: A Community Zine*—the last of which has raised over $1,000 for abortion resources. When they're not writing, S.R. enjoys reading, rock climbing, and film photography.

{contents}

Jules Kontozissi-Dahlstrom

Boy With Hair Tie on Wrist

It's sick geometry, the way my straight edges parallel curves.
I can't do long division; can't make separations
or distinctions. Can't write definitions.
I can stand in the middle indecisively, wandering
on the cusp of binary. In the seventh grade,
I failed algebra
because I couldn't understand the slope of my body
and why the equation was different every day. Why
I could do all the math the boys did
and never get the same answer.

I used to want to major in math before
I realized it is all numbers. I couldn't understand why
I had to be quantifiable. Had to be finite.
Or why I had to keep my arms at certain angles
to be considered rational. Why I had to be either
positive or negative
to be real. But I did know for a fact
that I was always solvable. Boy with hair tie on wrist
girl with jungled legs. I can't do long division
but I can add until I die. Can't label quadrilaterals but
I can build the 3D models. I used to want to major
in math before I realized it's all facts—
except for the fact
that it's all theory.

Slone Leman

Wallet Poem

The old-new, real leather, engraved wallet swallows my hands,
and I'm lost in the folds.
One day it'll belong to me, but it will never belong to me
like it could have.

My mother says that everybody feels the same way they did when they were kids
and she's positively stumped when I say that I've done nothing but change.
Something asks if I'm not just changing, but rotting in places,
stuck in a scramble to dig out the mold
but I wave whatever it is away before i get to thinking
about that damn wallet.

"What's so important about it anyway?"
I'm always saying, like I don't know
how good it would feel to wrap a coarse hand around the leather
like we're made of the same material
to give it, sitting in my back pocket, a hearty slap
like a man should.

Pui C.

Where the Heart Isn't

You picked up photography as a hobby. You have a paralyzing fear
of forgetting. These may or may not be correlated.

They say the first thing you forget about someone is their voice.
You still remember your first muse's voice when she sang / when
she sang you praises / when she sang you to sleep in your dreams
but you forget the texture of her hands. The same way you do not
realize you've forgotten the texture of the shelves, of the wall-
papers in the house you grew up in. The cabinet may have been
purple but you cannot be sure. You'd always disliked purple.

You'd always been unhappy too. Or just never feeling, never living,
never real. Not in the house that you're sure would seem smaller and
humbler and simply *neutral* if you ever could go back, but you can't,
and you can't stop thinking about it, and you can't stop thinking
why you're thinking about it. Why, when your life has never been
better now that you've left– now that you *never again* have to stare at
the ceiling in the dark *never again* forced to listen to your mother's
snores and songs from another time *never again* from the radio at
the end of your mother's bed *never again*.

You had never been truly happy
there, but at least you knew the floor tiles by heart, and like a paint-
er you could recreate them perfectly behind your eyes. Yesterday
for the first time it struck you that you can't quite tell what shades
of brown the tiles were anymore.

You picked up photography not as a result but as a hobby. There
is never a reason for you to take photos of your own home but you
picked up photography as a hobby so now you take more pictures at
each place you go to than you ever did in

the seaside cell you spent half-thirty rotting in. There are no pho-
tos of the bedroom that was never yours / no photos of the piano
you used to hide under / no photos of the bathroom you so often
fantasized about dying in *there are no photos* and you are forget-
ting and you have a paralyzing fear of forgetting and you simply
cannot remember

what color the bed frame was.

Jules Kontozissi-Dahlstrom

O Brawling Love!

Juliet, I knew you were beautiful.
Sometimes, when I am away from the beautiful, the womanly,
I second-guess myself.
But there, I saw you, all pink and white,
reds like the forever stabbing beating of the heart
There I saw you draped and veiled and beautiful,
and I have never wanted anything more than to be beautiful.

Sometimes, I stray; mingle with the Montagues
And the slope of Romeo's nose
the smallest rugged scar
the lock of golden-brown or
the freckle of sun and strength
catches me in a war, and I realize
I have never wanted anything more than to be strong.

I was born naked, and then the choice was stolen from me—
and the Capulets lock the doors
of the Capulet household
And I am on one side on the fence,
and I will die on this side of the fence.
Mother knows best.

Do I dare to cross? The red of blood
and the blue of tears,
Is it not all the same, blending in a haze to make violet petals—
is it not all the same?
I was born under this name, but both sides of the fence
are just land to walk on—to graze like sheep
What am I crossing
if not an imaginary line
made of small angers and human ideas?

In the center is a dirt road,
a path to break in alone
streaked with purple mud
and amethyst blossoms
On my crown is a sheer veil, rose and delicate
at my feet are navy blue boots, golden-brown buckles

as I walk, plucking clover like harp strings,
I am carving
defiance: a new name.

gabriel matthews

desecrated.

you, my dear, have ruined me for good.

you've made me decay
in a way no lover would dare.

and while i sit here,

decomposing from inside out,

you stare,

and smile that rotting smile,

taunting me
with a craving i'll never satisfy.

Gabriela Murray

mirena

the women who   crawl out of my ballpoint pen
          have shadows for eyes and   bleeding for lips
they whisper in great globs of twilight   i should

          i should

turn on the tv bathe in the static and the   stuttering spotlight
          wend ocular nerve   into wire begging for
     your   junk skeleton sternum's   kinked protrusion
                    bring the bony chalk to my tongue   as if i couldn't be a nave
                    taste the copper rod   too bright and alien   to know

                    loose crimson   in the warm place where crimson is   should not
be

               the little girl   inside the big wet red smile   across the
     soft pale excess of   my   gut makes   lace   out of capillaries and
          scratches
               slogans   into the   pleural space   with her   small keratins
     words scramble off
                                   our
                                        property   your object
my   moral dripping hands

          the   arterial silence   gushes warm like a   fever   we   are
     a sanguine   mucous sunshower
                         on tile floor

          eat from me   endometrium-darling
                                             the yarrow   moon
     says
               it   won't be long
                                        now

Linus Elkins

A man at the bus stop asks me if I'm trans

That is to say a man at the bus stop asks of an apple why it tempts
and not why there should be shame in what's tempting,
makes me want to ask him why I should answer to a line in the sand,
I'd much like to wield what drew it,
was it your finger? See how I have hands too,
we haven't lived so different.

Linus Elkins
LADY! IN FRONT OF ME ON THE TRAIN

The light rail to school is a social space
under the expectation of zero communing.
Immaturity! No one budges for no one!
Would you agree? Lady with the faux leather
jacket that chips at the shoulder! Lady with
the one gray strand that needles through the hole
in your beret! I hope the moths in your wardrobe
retire to an island. When I was younger I thought
the trailers they used to transport horses in were
hilarious. To watch them silent in that sardine tin.
Watch me now! I'm a fool. I'm a foal. And
you've got a little hole in your yellow beret.

Edd Rugg

N.B.

Them

the third eyes
spinning on wheels
which spill visions
of carnivorous women
block veins
like thin-skinned
climate nuts
and turn pulse
into gruel,
thick,
spoon stuck standing

the heartless bastard
s
they have no
definition
s
are
shapeless
s
ghouls
they live at night
and move in
alcoholic gaggles s
hissing
they will get you
eventually

gabriel matthews

untitled (aka a poem about polyamory and outer space)

he[1] is my sun,

he[2] is my moon,

he[3] is my stars,

and i[4] am the earth.

[1] golden and glowing / sending warmth and care / through the solar system / for all to see
[2] tranquil and tantalizing / guiding the night / with its celestial glow / for all to see
[3] serene and stunning / populating every corner / of the dark sky / for all to see
[4] awestruck / as i have the privilege / to be caught in the midst / of such beauty.

Slone Leman

Soften

You're a hopeless romantic,
you know that the plastic star
dangling from the rearview can save you.
It swings back and forth pendulum style,
as the bus driver maneuvers snaking mountain bends
and you tuck your knees up
against the faux leather seat in front of you.
You also know that the world will never love you back
in the way that you want it to.
Swirling angst,
and the unmistakable urge to listen to Green Day,
fill your stomach

You're a hopeless romantic.
Doe eyed staring up at the stars,
heart turned putty when fat raindrops make perfect circles on your t-shirt.
But nowadays, the world outside seems to remind you
of something else.
Constellations look less like
relics of the past (forever out of your grasp)
and more like the freckles dotting his neck.
He loves Green Day
so your anger associated with Billie Joe's howling
melts away.

You're still a hopeless romantic,
though you're older than you ever thought you'd get.
You didn't need
a flimsy plastic star
to save you.
You and him have broken up,
or stayed together.
It doesn't really matter.
You know that the world will never love you back
and you let your brow soften
when you see the stars
anyway.

Lily Healy

Carmilla, I want…

I want you to crash your car and climb from the wreckage
only to drag me in with you as the engine explodes;
the flames chill our bones and we will feel
what it's like to leave the house.

I want you to lie about your birthday
so I feel better lying about my name.
We are both terrible people deserving of hell
but no one deserves where we'll end up.

I want to stay home from school today
because I had a dream about the man in my wall.
He has a destiny laid out for me in the kitchen
and said the steak knives would feel so
lovely in my chest.
He carved a wooden knife just for you, Carmilla,
will you stay home too?

I want you to grow your nails long
so I can paint them every color on the sidewalk.
I want puncture wounds on my cheeks
so people will stop looking at my eyes.
I want blood to pour from my skin
so I'll never run out of blush.
I want to forget how to scab
because it's a useless skill anyway.

I want to know what it's like for your hands to wring my neck and
I want to stop focusing on my breath and
I want you to want to kill me.
Nobody's ever cared enough to kill me.

Mia-Jo Feeley

DESCRIPTION OF A SUBURB

If the Earth had psychosis, it would
be the golf course; a great hole at the core
of everything. The atrophy & entropy
of capital. Here, your name is the speed

limit. Your dreams are air-conditioned nightmares,
and who can say we didn't try? No one.
Not through the haze of strawberry bubblegum
nicotine clouds, the hemorrhage we call

present, the algorithm arthritis, I'm
not the one to say where to go from here, but
let me orbit the real, the gentle & unbearable real.
The truth is not at the bottom of

a coffee cup, but I am & I am washed
clean in this Starbuck's bathroom sink

Micah Buchman

If beetles stood the way we stood, head facing upwards, they'd always be in a state of prayer

the top of the head is a godly place
but human is fungi in the gut, leg hair, being called
a borer.
dance in your drag names:
horn's fairy shrimp hunting, devil's coach horse, transvestite rove,

divine in your tarsal
formula, your mothers frozen in amber.
the fossil record states that
drowning in bark rot is good
for evolution and for the soul

that we are meant to branch off into horseshoe crabs and
furry elk, that you are meant to be
both photographed and left alone
that i was meant to sit alone in a museum half-transitioned
and recite the amidah

rat king
by Carter Kirby

rat king /ˈrat kiŋ/

noun

a collection of rats whose tails are intertwined and bound together in some way.

sometimes, i felt that way about you, like
we were just two little creatures
who played too much, too hard
in something too sticky
and then we were

tangled up

the thing
about rat kings
is that no one ever
makes it out alive
they all start pulling in different
directions, or attacking each other
i don't know who to blame for how we got this way
but what i do know is that sometimes
i really hate you

i have always been,
so goddamn
independent
and, usually,
when you love someone,
finally opening up
is freeing
like a door swung open,
revealing all the
fresh air
and foliage
off the front porch
but, with you
it felt more like
a dissection
invasive
and uninvited
like i was strapped
to operation tables
hissing with
each incision
and still,
in the mirror sometimes,
i see the scars, grit my teeth,
and then
i wonder
if the rats feel this way too, like
"we can keep clawing at
each other's faces
even if it only makes things worse
because we're stuck together
and i'm sick of you
i'm sick of the way you drag me
across the subway floor
im sick of being followed into
every room
im sick of alone having lost
all it's meaning"

i wonder when it was that we both understood / the only way out of a rat king / is to chew off your tail / we had to have both been thinking / "which one of us is gonna do it?"/ when we both know, i'm the only one / with teeth sharp enough to / gnaw away at any part of anyone / i'm the only one with the guts / to take a seam ripper / to the places that we've been sewn together / after the break up / while i scrub the last hickey you gave me / off of my neck / i tally all the ways i tried to make it work / and all the ways you didn't / do good people do that? i think / probably not / but i don't think i get to be the victim / in every one of my poems / not every word out of my mouth / is as pretty as the ones i put on paper / maybe after months of pulling you off the train tracks / it's my turn to take the rope / you haven't exactly been a saint either / and, call me vengeful, but i feel / at least a little bit / like i deserve this, or, / i deserved all of it

Celia McClure-Sikkema

Shitstain on Swimsuit

Sunspots / like leopard print / peeking out of / sky blue / one piece / crepe thighs / big / rust / seeping into quick dry fabric / two grandsons / you are beautiful / lifetime of beach trips and brushing teeth cloaked in chlorophyll / I am 20 / and staring / lilac colored bikini and pink claws / I spent two hours worth of pay to get rid of fine lines / smile lines / L and I sandwich M / the blondes / the first two faces / two years in now / and I still can't believe / I get to eat chips on the beach / with pretty girls I love / out of the blue / falling from the sky / I blurt / how many kids do you guys want / I'm trying to think / how many towels will we need in twenty years?

Micah Buchman

the diatom chain and their redness

and He
created silica
and the rivers that house
silica and the hymns to silica
i split from His everythingness
and then in the present
silica sleepy
day,

i build a
glass house
on a whale's
skin and float
to the market
with my multiples
we form a fan
and sing old
folk as i eat
chili almonds
and i write a new
coping statement;
my body is joy
too, envy is not
my river,

and
i know i am right
because we write reciprocal
odes about each others' shapes
we create our own energy and we
hold each others' pinkies regardless
we pool our money and feed our pools
we see through each others' opaline
and still say i love you and
grow larger than He ever
imagined

mars

less than jacob

the biggest battle in the war was against peace,
the peace keeping everyone in the dark,
complacent,
ready to jump if it meant the eternal reward
of the pastor's praise.
we raged against it in the dark,
unable to disturb the slumbering beast
that was silent, heavy peace.
our first rebellion was not an act, but a lacking,
filling the contribution dish with uncomfortable nothing,
the communion cups left in their unholy place
on the golden platter of lying greed,
exponential growth made possible by the tithe,
the ten percent of my time spent gazing at the stage
and hoping they cannot see the way i escape my rage
through the emptiness in my eyes.
the war was on love, on community and trust
and unbreakable bonds
which vanish when the rules are not followed.
the friendships never broke off but faded,
pulled away when someone dared to question
whether or not we were the victims
or the perpetrators of the uncomfortable judgment
hanging heavy in the air around those
who had not yet committed their lives
to the word of man, regarding the lord.
the double-edged sword of damocles that hung over us,
threatening to send us to the same place as those we preached to
if we stepped over the thin white line of mana separating our high school auditori-
um
from the corrupted world outside
if we forgot our holy place above the sinners
we were tasked with turning to our greedy Lord.
we were told to multiply, bring in two who would bring two of their own
until the whole world was one under the word of the lord
and that of the men who gathered us.
the pastor's wife told me to give up that which held me back
and i found that i was not held back by the darkness
but pushed away from the light.

it was the realization that the peace was impenetrable,
that i would fade from before their pearly gates in silence
which let me turn my back and leave the front lines
of my battle with the lord's people.
you cannot beat a force of hope
even if the faith is hellbent on crushing you beneath its boot
without a second fucking thought.
i stay in the shadows and warn people from them
and hope that maybe i save someone else
from the fate i faced,
caught in a bear trap staring down the blade
of the gospel
and the hatred that wields it.

gabriel matthews

orison for the regretful

i clasp my hands
and i cough out a prayer
or maybe it's blood
       (i was never very good at telling the difference)
these words feel thick and
almost heavy
like an admission of guilt
       (but really, what is prayer if not for the guilty?)
 i've reached a point where i
can't tell if this prayer is for
me, or G-d, or you
       (and at this point, does it even matter?)
and, if i'm being honest,
this is less of a prayer
and more of a plea
       (a not-so-important distinction)
a plea as penance
a plea to be absolved
a plea for a return to the way things were before
       (a plea to say that i'm sorry.)

Milo Hodges

My Top Surgeon is God and I am an Atheist

I have never been my own.
Abnormal amalgamation, an afterthought
I am the synthesis you fear.
I detest you. You're all that I've got.

You cradle my ribs,
Intercept my faithless prayers.
Ask me your questions. Please, don't make me stare.

Aren't you the salt of the earth?
The light of a candlestick, righteous and holy
Blessed be the man, sworn under oath

You set the star in the east and sat right underneath.
Did you think I'd rejoice, for salvation without regret?

I am the only man in this room.
You saved my life. I may never forgive you.

Push my eyes closed with reverent fingertips
You reshape me, enrage me, I'm thankful.
Tried to dissuade me, or blame me - disengage.
Now I can live with my dagger in my cloak

Am I of your own image?
Created in your likeness,
Clay in the hands of the potter

You think you know me by my fruits,
but I have thistles nestled in my tissue.

You could not see my hunger, you thirsted for proof
Yet for my faithlessness, I bear the guilt
My body may be yours, but I hold on to my soul
My own mercy, that I pray I am worthy of.

I yearn for the sweetness of forgetting
I marvel at the dove eating the lark
Your beloved son, in whom you are well pleased
Dear God, I was only fifteen.

Edd Rugg

punk rockers for jesus

can i just ask
u
show respect?
fuck me not
with dirty words
like,
"God",
or
Bother
me not with combs me
not with christ-like false
teeth.
blinding
white and full of shit.

let us not hang today
refuse the
hankering bells
that strike
under water
cankering odd

ideas or dylan thomas'
filthy metaphysics.

i will not dance today
with the dolphins

this is not anger
this is marmite
you mother fucker

so choose
a
bleeding
heart
sew it to your nearest sleeve

i only ask
you show respect
and shave it off
when it's time
to fuck...

Pui C.

Affairs of the Heart: a combination of both the Truth Game and Murder

tear ducts like a milk tooth tied to a doorknob: slam the wood,
it comes flying
                out; a few droplets. do a somersault.
breathe in the dust and blow out the candles: count the
        particles tainted by your spit count the syllables tainted
by your sanity; count the
        ears you mar with a truth delivered in slivers of your
heart. dear heart,
                        proximity
        is a privilege i wish i could unlearn to love. how lucky a
palm, singed by the glow of your wrath; how
        lucky a tongue, caught in the flames of your spite; how
lucky an arm, gashed by the blunt of your claws, praise be.
the glory in crossfire wounds, the honor of having
        heaven
                in an arm's reach.

a slow learner knows to recite the silhouette of your
indifference; a slow-dancer learns to crush her feet before the
tango starts.

Footnote: This is a reference to The Boys In The Band, a 1968 play by Mart Crowley
that was revived on Broadway in 2018 and adapted into films. "Affairs of the Heart
is a combination of both the Truth Game and Murder– with a new twist."

Ahmad Faisal

Critic

The critic stood still,
sharpened his swords, killed the poem.
He accused the poet of ignorance.
The poet would die if his knowledge got lost.
People would die if they lost their loved ones.
'Your poem is flawed. You repeated 'I'
more than twenty times
as if the jinn in al-Mutanabbi's poetry
knows the jinn in yours.'
The poet replied,
'I have the right to be arrogant.
I described her eyes in just a line.
My fingers dared to touch the keyboard
to write Beloved, I want to taste you without being guilty.'
The keyboard is shut down, I go to bed.
It sends my beloved a morning text:
The lovely thing about you, your sharp features.
The beautiful thing about me, I love sharpness.
The worst thing about our journey, it ends.
The best thing about our journey, I see you.
My heart drops off to stop the train wheels
to prolong the journey,
leaving a window in the rib cage to look at you.
When you notice, it averts,
pretending to be blind as if you were a princess.
I might die breathless.
You assassinated my modest poem
hidden deep down in my easy heart,
ordering my fingers to hit the keyboard.
I was arrogant when I crafted an image for you.
I repeated the 'I' twenty times,
allowing the critic to accuse me of ignorance.

Silas Kollmer

untitled

All these ghosts dwell here.
  Don't go here, turn around turn around
This house is theirs. Reno is theirs. They aren't my mother. They aren't my mother.
  This place doesn't welcome you, turn around turn around
As I approached, my head grew light - like I was about to faint. My body ached. I
had to lie down and never rise again. Now I can't sleep.
  This is not a kind place for you. This is not yours
  Turn around turn around
This was never home, it never felt like home, it always felt like a coffin. The second
the old carpet was pulled up, the second the drywall was painted, we never could
get the smell of sulfur out -
  Do you remember what you last saw here?
  Did you forget our scorched earth?
  Turn around turn around
They say the land is cursed, a house torn to shreds by greed on the hill, burnt to a
crisp in search of precious, perfect copper.
  Nothing happens without a cause
  Turn around turn around
I've spent two years in this prison, screamed cried bled puked until it sapped every
inch of me into a hollow shell. Two years with no one but my brain, nothing but a
blue screen and this godforsaken city, nothing but a blue room in the back of this
godforsaken house. Two years of brown and gray, two years of horses and green
checked sheets, two years of loneliness-
  This is not for you anymore
  Turn around turn around
Did the desert know how it dried me from the inside? Did the beige bathroom tile
crack when her heart died and she fell onto it? Did the smell of sulfur ever go away?
Do windchimes still sing in the spring, is the city still coated in a layer of dark filth,
are there still the casinos clouded by cigarette smoke, do the bugs still fly into
people's hair?
  You feel this for a reason
  Turn around turn around
Does any of it still remember how she died? Does any of it still remember her?
  Do you know us?
  Did anyone ever know us?
  Does anyone ever think of us?
  Is this a blessing or a curse?
  Turn around turn around
What is one more ghost to a land full of them?
Leave us alone

Yatharth Rajput
On Salt and Rust

we are
  run of the mill
does
  looking for prey

oh it's so funny
  the year will end
before we all do
  and yet
we'll make it work
  once again

oh, love
  is embarrassing
the human race
  i love it

push october mist
  infected with
rust & salt
  and a pack of saltines
that you left
  on the couch – into my throat
and i will stop
  fighting
this surrender

i burn out candles
  to smoke up
this entire place:
  in here i mean

if our nail paint is chipped
  and teeth start
tightening around
  nothingness it is because we
have finally found it
  in its whole form:
love – green and earthy

november rain becomes splinters
  giving into gravity and still we look up
with our slit wrist & stilt supported bodies
  & stilled bruises don't you understand
to love is to become the rain

we travelled miles
  only to come
back to our mothers & fathers
  don't you
understand how
far we go
  just to stay this close

Indigo Smith

Cannonballing Past the Event Horizon

I stand on the sidewalk, a shivering, sedate candle flame in a camp sweatshirt,
waiting for my friend to pick me up

it's dark, only soft slices of the
rosy-Creamsicle-colored streetlights providing sporadic relief
and my friend is fourteen minutes late
and bitterness and terror dance past me right next to the howling wind

these are the parts that get to me
that tear ragged the edges of my lungs
and press bruises into places I can't even see
these parts before and after, alone, they flood my eyes greyscale
I fiddle with my hoodie strings, trying not to cave in and cry

but then, down the sharp, inky expanse of road,
a snowy spark appears just below the horizon
and grows, splitting into two artificial suns that announce the end of the before
and the world's vibrance returns like a painkiller kicking in

my friend pulls up beside me, and I pop in as fast as I can
she sets us on our way to our destination,
and the whole world's right here, isn't it?

words drift between us like
iridescent bubbles,
and I don't know if anything I'm saying is
particularly true, but we left that distinction behind way back
there's no room for it
we can only fit her and I and the music,
swirling out of the speakers, the tempo making pace for our heartbeats

"We're bending the world around us, like a black hole," I tell her. "It's a lot more
pleasant than I imagined."

"Well," she replies, her eyes gleaming into the windshield, her form painted with
streaky neon, "I don't know why everyone's so scared of the
inside of a black hole.
They're black because
they keep

all the light they've ever touched
and they hold it inside themselves
so if you went in, all that starlight
would be right there
and wouldn't that be beautiful?"

I say, "hell yeah,"

and a new song comes on
and the shell of the car shakes with our singing as it carries us forward,
our gravity warping the taillights behind us
as we become ever more full,
letting nothing go.

Mia-Jo Feeley

HEAVEN IS THE GAY CLUB (PLAY OUR SONG)

When we die, I hope we break it
down. Break it like bread. Eat what's left
of Heaven. Leave no crumbs.

I hope we play chicken
in a street with no cars, spin
on chrome poles, take a shot. Aim for the stars.

The Seraphim play in stereo. It's all SOPHIE
from here to the Big Bang.
Give it the full moon of your attention,

your curled, solar flare hair; prominence
& filaments of your nuclear heart.
Your heart that makes atoms anew, water into wine

& better miracles. Miracle of arithmetic.
Miracle of eclipse: the diameters of sun and moon,
the impossible inevitable:

that we would meet, & meet again.
When we die, we will meet again.
Of course. In a world of bullets,

hook your body to whatever holds it!
Let the police pour in, pour one out
and watch them drown.

Friend! My snare drum heart is yours
to beat on the Senate steps.
Let us be fact, and if we burn, let us

be tinder! Let their inferno be our
Paradiso! Let their law fall on our skulls,
and we'll see who breaks first.

{ contributors }

Mia-Jo Bella is a trans poet from Tulsa, OK, and an alumna of Amplify Tulsa's Youth Leadership Council for sexual health advocacy. She's interested in nurturing a future for trans people.

Micah Robert Marks Buchman is a nineteen-year-old New Yorker residing in Claremont, California. He creates collages about transgender existence and God, kisses his friends on the mouth, and loves people-watching on the subway. His poems have been featured in The Agave Review and Potluck.

Pui C. (they/them) is a bibliophile who writes to preserve their sanity. They grew up in Hong Kong, do amateur photography, and love their friends. They are currently working on falling in love with life.

Born and raised in Seattle, **Linus Elkins** is a poet, writer, and proud owner of a library card.

Ahmad Faisal is an aspiring, award-winning Egyptian poet. In 2022, he was awarded the State Award for Young Innovators. Faisal has authored two poetry collections: Toys Seller (2022) and A Cup of Friska Tea (2022).

Lily Healy is an college student majoring in astronomy, writing poetry whenever she can in her free time.

Milo Hodges is nineteen, and a trans, classical guitarist who likes to write poetry.

Carter Kirby (they/them) is a queer, trans poet, actor, and activist based outside of Little Rock, Arkansas, known for their self published zines and spoken word work, as well as community organizing and graphic design with Lemon Pepper Poetry Slam and the Committee of Labor for Arkansas Workers (CLAW).

Silas Kollmer loves queer history, writing, and his little fluffy dog Evie. He lives in San Francisco.

Jules Kontozissi-Dahlstrom has been recognized in numerous competitions such as TheaterWorksUSA and CT Student Writers Magazine. Other than a poet, Jules is a Greek-American, an artist, a community member, and a lover. In his writing, he hopes to illustrate the human experience in its rawest form—even when it isn't beautiful.

Slone Leman is a trans poet and musician based in British Columbia. They are a high school student hoping to pursue writing and music after graduation.

mars is an autistic, transmasc poet from massachusetts who writes about his life, love, heartbreaks and trauma. it is a proud dog dad, queer rights advocate, and dedicated lover. he began writing at 13 as a way to let others understand his feelings, and never plans to stop.

gabriel matthews (he/him) is gay, trans, and somewhat menacing. he's a lover of anything strange, unusual, or uncomfortable. he is based in rural nevada.

Celia McClure-Sikkema is a Social Work student and poet in Michigan. They enjoy connecting with creatures in nature, and falling in love. Their poems "perma-valentine", "Growth//Decay", "separation", and "we wake up in the summer" have been featured in Proud to Be–A Pride Poetry Collection, published by The Red Penguin Collection.

Gabriela Murray is a student at Bard College who believes in lesbianism, celestiality, and the nonbinary applications of Judaism.

Yatharth Rajput, an emerging creative writer from India, is a passionate poet, storyteller, and memoirist whose work focuses on contemporary themes. His eloquent verse delves into the intricacies of marginalized experiences as a person of colour, intersectionality, family dynamics, forgiveness, anger, , the working adult, language and semantics.

Edd Rugg (they/she/he) lives in England, where they study History, read poetry and desperately try to remember meat is murder in between crashing in and out of doors (dyspraxic)

Indigo Smith is a silly guy who lives in Washington State. They love cats, space, almond croissants, learning too many languages, and making horrible puns. They watch the film Tangled approximately once every 80 days.

9 798990 348820